What is a paladin?

A paladin is a holy warrior dedicated to the power of Law and the cause of Good. They right wrongs, defend the innocent, and thwart evil.

Many people think that Law and Good are limits on your power. In fact, Law and Good ARE your power.

"Law" is more than a set of rules.
It is the idea that consistent standards of
behaviour help to make you more organized,
more reliable, and more effective as a person.

Every paladin has a Code, a series of precepts that make you a better warrior. Write your Code down, think about it, refine it, and then commit to it.

"Good" is more than being nice. It is a dedication to truth, justice, helping those who need help, and making the world, objectively, a better place.

When you honestly, legitimately care about others
and their well-being, Good comes naturally.

Every paladin's Code is different, but they usually have the most important things in common:

Bring aid to those who cannot defend themselves.
Ensure that those who do evil face the
consequences of their actions.
Respect legitimate authority.
Tell the truth.
Be consistent.

Being consistent is important. A paladin who only
follows their Code part-time is not a real paladin.

Dedicating yourself to your Code every day is very difficult.
But it is worth it.

It is important to remember that Good is the purpose for which you fight, and Law is the most effective weapon in that fight. Sometimes, Good and Law will appear to be in conflict. When that happens, Good should trump Law.

These apparent conflicts do not mean that
Law is ineffective or that it should be abandoned.
They just mean that life is complicated and no one
Code can ever be adaptable enough to handle it all.
That's okay.

Sometimes, you'll meet paladins who do things differently than you do. Maybe their Code doesn't look like yours. Maybe they use different weapons. Maybe they follow a different god, or no god at all. It is important to respect them as fellow warriors for the cause of Good.

Sometimes, you'll meet people who fight on your side,
but who are not paladins. They might be able to do
things that you cannot. As long as you work together
for a common goal, they can be valuable allies.
(Even if they're not as effective or as dedicated as you are.)

It is important to take care of yourself.
If you eat properly, sleep regularly, and
maintain your equipment, you will be a more
effective holy warrior. Making sure that you
are the best paladin you can be is not selfish.

A dull blade is an asset to your enemy.
Stay sharp.

Appearance is important. Paladins
should be clean, organized, well-equipped,
and appear ready at all times to help.

If you appear heroic, people who
need a hero will come to you.
(This is what you want.)

At any given time, you should always be able to answer the questions "What are you doing?" and "Why are you doing that?".

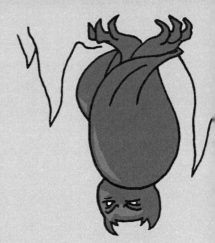

When you enter a new area,
always remember to look up.

If you encounter a creature or phenomenon you don't recognize, ask an expert's opinion before you do anything.

Paladins always give generously to charity. They donate time, resources, and money to people and organizations that help the needy, even if it's not in their personal best interests.

Always research the charity
thoroughly before you donate.

If someone is cowering, crying, and begging
for mercy, you have to stop hitting them.
This is not up for debate.

If someone is cowering, crying, and begging for mercy,
you have to stop your teammates from hitting them.
This is not up for debate.

If someone says they are hungry, feed them.
If someone says they are hurt, give them medical attention.
If someone says they are cold, warm them up.

This does not mean that
you have to trust them.

If you can get yourself a big impressive sword, go for it. The shinier, the better.

Make sure that if you lose your big shiny sword, you can still fight.

Scaring someone or threatening to hurt
them will usually make them tell you what
they think you want to hear, or misinformation
that they think will hurt you.

Showing someone that you genuinely want to make their lives better or to help their loved ones is a good way to get legitimate, useful information.

Never split the party.

Never trust statues.

Sometimes, you will feel sad. That is okay.

Sometimes, you will feel frustrated. That is okay.

Sometimes, you will feel
worn out. That is okay.

If you feel sad, frustrated or worn out for a long time, it is okay to talk to somebody about it. Getting help is the responsible thing to do.

Every paladin should have a big, booming, powerful voice that carries well and is impossible to ignore. Practice it regularly.

Use your powerful voice to:
Accuse corrupt leaders of wrongdoing
Announce the victories and achievements of your team
Proclaim the universal principles of Good and Law
Celebrate

Every paladin should have a quiet, intense, serious voice that does not carry, but is impossible to ignore. Practice it regularly.

Use your intense voice to:
Accuse teammates of wrongdoing
Accept blame and admit failure
Make promises
Mourn

Honest speech is effective speech.
If you develop a reputation for always telling
the truth and keeping your promises, it will
make people more likely to listen to you.

Honesty is inconvenient, but it is worth it.
If you cannot be honest, be silent.

Some people are not as good at communicating as others. Maybe they have a thick accent or a limited vocabulary. Maybe they stutter. Maybe they're just not very charismatic.

That just means you have
to listen more carefully.

Heal others, then yourself.

Remember to heal yourself.

You cannot fight evil if you don't encounter evil. Seek it out. Keep your eyes open.

You cannot protect the innocent if you don't encounter the innocent. Seek them out. Keep your heart open.

Everything you own should have a specific purpose.

"Because it makes me happy" is a valid purpose.

Sometimes, you'll rescue
townsfolk, and they won't reward you.
Rescue them anyway.

Sometimes, you'll rescue townsfolk,
and they won't even thank you.
Rescue them anyway.
(Maybe leave town, though.)

Every paladin can fall.

Every fallen paladin can be redeemed.

Be merciful.
Be helpful.
Be noble.
Be trustworthy.
Be effective.
Be heroic.

Be lawful.
Be good.

-About the Authours-

Alaren "Big Al" Dendrakos is a celestial-blooded paladin of Celeric the All-Seeing. He favours the longsword and has a talent for healing magic. He has been adventuring for five years with various groups, has vanquished more monsters than he can count, and has saved an entire kingdom from being taken over by evil forces at least twice. He has fallen, and has been redeemed.

Bembobimbom "Beebee" Littlewhistle is a halfling bard who has worked with Big Al for three years. She sings, she dances, she tells tales, and - in this case - she writes and draws. Beebee has also helped save kingdoms.

Mason "Tailsteak" Williams is a Canadian cartoonist, primarily known for his webcomics One Over Zero and Leftover Soup. He has not saved any kingdoms to date.